Spirit of El Paso

The Sergeant Joe

Saldivar Story

By Michelle Murray

Printed in the United States of America

KMP Entertainment (Publishing Division)
www.kmpentertainment.org

The following story is based on the life of

Sergeant Joe Saldivar, of the El Paso County

Sheriff's Office, in El Paso, Texas. Some

characters, events and dialogue have been

dramatized for a more intriguing tale.

Chapter One

Jesús looks at the calendar on his bedroom wall. It is Thursday, May 29, 1947. One more day before he will surprise his wife, Esperanza, with tickets to Cine Plaza, the beautiful new theater on Av. 16 De Septiembre. It opened on the day his son Joe was born two months ago on March 19th. Things have been a bit busy, caring for three children, to say the least. Jesús and his wife haven't had any opportunities to spend time alone. He misses that.

Just then, he hears a loud crack. He feels it, too. Everyone in the home feels it shake. His wife runs in with the children, clutching baby Joe next to her chest. The other two children still toddlers, hold onto the hem of her dress. Metal rains down, crashing into their roof.

"Stay put. I'll go see what's happening," Jesús assures Esperanza.

He grabs his hat and coat, then dashes toward the front door. Two of the windows shatter as the house continues to shake. Jesús pauses for a moment, then grabs his sidearm from the closet shelf. Just in case.

He opens the door to chaos. People run in every direction. Women scream inf fear as children squeal with delight while the men of the Ascensión Municipality in Juarez, Mexico try to figure out what is going on. As he takes in the scene, Jesús notices a friend who calls out to him.

"Maybe a UFO, Jesús? I'm not sure what it is, but look!"

The man points down a hill toward Tepeyac Cemetery. Jesús eyes a smoldering crater that is some twenty four feet deep and fifty feet wide.

"Ay, Dios Mío!"

Jesús has no idea what he is looking at, nor do the other men who are gathering. Metal fragments still rain down intermittently upon them.

"Do you know what time it is? I'm going to call this in to the police. They'll want to know what time all this started."

"It's seven thirty PM," Jesús starts.

Then he hesitates. No, it's not.

"Actually, that's what time my watch stopped," he continues.

Some of the other men glance at their watches. They are also at a standstill. The men nervously look around to each other. One man moves closer to the crater. He stoops down and picks up a few charred fragments.

"I'm going to head home, but I'll take a souvenir to my wife," he says.

The other men give an uneasy chuckle.

"Yeah, my wife will want some sort of souvenir," Jesús' friend shares as he, too, rummages through the dirt to find something of value.

There are some steel tanks, and some sort of wiring. He also sees some spun wool.

"I can put these tanks and wiring to use to make some model planes with my boy. He has a fascination with those things. What about this wool? It's wet, but do you want it, Jesús?"

"Sure. Maybe my wife can make *ME* a souvenir. A sweater or something."

The men break into an uneasy laughter just as the Federales arrive. Jesús and his friends tip their hats to one another and head in the direction of their homes. Both of the men are out of earshot when the warning is given by police to be wary of the spilled hydrogen peroxide and the spun wool insulation that has come from a V2 rocket.

The German V2 rocket is being studied and improved at White Sands Missile Range, about eighty miles north in the United States. Just two weeks before, one has been tested and launched, but it crashed violently in Alamogordo, New Mexico. The rocket that crashed and left the crater that Jesús and his friends witnessed is just as violent, if not more.

US Army officials have been hoping to have success with this rocket through the secret Hermes II program. The V2 rocket has been improved greatly from previous versions. The tail of the rocket that crashed in Juarez is much larger than others, and wings have been added to the top.

Despite the care taken to improve the rocket, it still has some guidance issues and barreled into Juarez at supersonic speed, over 2,000 miles per hour, crashing pointy end first, making the large crater Jesús has seen.

The next day, newspapers in the US report the rocket's impact is equal to the 1,800 pound warhead explosive the rocket would have carried a few years prior during World War II. The El Paso Times' front page is covered with photos, news reports and explanations from various military officials. In addition, there is an opinion piece basically saying that the crash was "too close for comfort," and citing the potential hazards, like cancer, that could result.

Jesús and his family go on about their lives and don't see any of that news coverage. Within a year, the family welcomes a baby daughter and a doctor has diagnosed Jesús with cancer. Within two years, Jesús is dead and his family moves to El Paso, Texas.

Chapter Two

Esperanza marries Simon Bustamante, a World War II Army Veteran, just after Joe's third birthday. The couple eventually welcomes a daughter of their own. Simon works hard to take care of his wife and the five kids who keep the house lively. Esperanza isn't too happy with the amount of liquor Simon consumes, but she stays quiet. Her life, and the children's, will be far better if she stays here in the United States. Addressing the alcohol will only serve to disrupt their now stable life. Besides, he was so good to the kids. He and Joe had a close relationship, probably better than her own relationship with her son. Things were rough after Jesús died, and she remembers…

"I see the Soviet Union launched something into space. I think they are calling it Sputnik. I hope we don't wind up in another war over this. World War Two. Korea. I don't want us in another one," Esperanza shares with Simon over breakfast.

He takes in this news and grimaces. He reaches for his coffee, then changes his mind.

"Hand me the tequila," he says to his wife, with an outstretched hand.

Esperanza eyes the children, then gets up to get the bottle from the highest shelf in the cabinet above the sink. The children take this as their cue to clear their plates and head out the door for school. Molly, the youngest, looks at her brother Joe and cries.

"You're just a baby. You can't go to school with us," Joe tells her before he bolts out the door to find his friends.

So begins most mornings. Breakfast and then spending the rest of the day pretending Simon is not an alcoholic; listening to his mother remind him what a good provider Simon is, and how lucky they all are to have this great war hero taking care of them.

Joe also has a wild side that he tames by constant partying. If there is any sort of house party, he is there. Even when Joe was as young as twelve or thirteen, he hung out with his friends, listened to music and drank as much alcohol as he could get his hands on.

By the time Joe is in the ninth grade at El Paso's Technical High, though, he's "over it."

"What do you mean you aren't coming back, Joe?" Chevo Quiroga, Joe's longtime friend asks in stunned disbelief.

"I mean: I am not coming back. I'm dropping out. Done. Outta here."

"You won't miss playing football? Eating lunch with us? Miss Galvan's history class?"

"Maybe Miss Galvan, but the rest of it? Nope!"

They boys let out a hearty laugh. Miss Galvan is one of the nicest teachers in the school. She is young, and she always cares about what you have to say. She's kind of like the big sister everyone wishes they had.

"And don't tell her I'm leaving," Joe commands Chevo.

"Why? She'll know you left when she sees your seat empty."

"I just don't want to have to explain."

"Well, at least explain to me," Chevo urges.

"I just want something more…"

And with that, he signs himself out in the school office for one final time, and never looks back.

Chapter Three

"Are you sure this is what you want to do, mijo? Move to California?"

Joe sighs. He is so sick of everyone asking him if this is what he wants to do. Yes. More than he wants to breathe. This is exactly what he wants to do. He's sixteen, for crying out loud! He can make his own decisions.

"Yes, Mother. I don't just want to do this. I need to do this. If I…"

A snore from across the room interrupts the conversation. It's only noon, but Simon has been drinking for hours, a Saturday morning ritual for him. Esperanza desperately wants him to talk Joe out of this move, talk him into going back to school, but she knows he won't. She feels insecure when she realizes Joe stares in amusement at Simon.

"He's a good provider…"

"I know. He's one of the good guys…"

Esperanza moves close to Joe and observes him for a moment. He has that same fiery look in his eye that his father, Jesús, had anytime he was determined to do something. Esperanza realizes she will not win this battle, so she softens.

"Your family will always be here for you. We love you. God be with you, son."

"I'll be back to visit. Soon. I promise."

"Do you have enough money?"

Joe has exactly zero dollars. He has spent all of his money from odd jobs hanging out with friends or buying things he doesn't need.

"No. That's why I've come to you. I need you to please give me the fifty dollars for the bus ticket to Sacramento."

Esperanza's jaw tightens.

"Absolutely not. I will not give you money to run off to California and do God knows what."

"Then I'll hop the train, like a hobo. I'll take my chances going for free then."

"I forbid it."

"I'm sixteen. I can do whatever I want."

"Not with my money, you won't."

"Well, like I said. I'll just hop the train and hope I don't get seen, or killed."

Esperanza thinks on this for a moment. She certainly does not wish to see harm come to her son. If only she could talk him out of this foolish decision! But she knows she cannot. Feeling defeated, she gets her purse from her bedroom. She rummages through it and fishes out sixty dollars.

"Here. Take this," Esperanza says as she tucks three twenty dollar bills into Joe's shirt pocket.

"I'll pay you back. I've already got a job lined up."

He does not have a job lined up. He has some ideas of where he will look, though.

"Why are you leaving again? What is wrong with our home here?"

Simon had purchased the home, near Trowbridge, for his family. It's modern and quite comfortable, unlike where many of their friends and family in Juarez live. They all feel blessed to live in comfort, always having enough. Joe especially feels grateful. But now that his brother is married and gone, and so is his older sister, it just doesn't feel like enough.

"I just want something more…"

By the time Joe rents a room at 1617 F Street in Sacramento, he is down to his last five dollars.

"Frijoles and rice and I'll be fine," Joe jokes to himself.

Fortunately, he is able to find a job immediately at The Mansion Inn. The restaurant's name has been chosen due to its close proximity to the Governor's home. The restaurant has several garden courtyards, multiple fountains, lavish plantings, a greenhouse and even a few pools.

"Your primary duties involve keeping the tables clean. You're going to clear all the dirty dishes and reset the tables with fresh linens."

Joe nods that he understands. The manager continues.

"I'll also need you to assist the servers during our lunch and dinner rushes."

"Assist the servers?" Joe asks.

"Yes. Refill drinks. Refill the condiments. Whatever help they need. Got it?"

Joe nods his head again.

"Well, get to work then. Bobby in the kitchen will show you where the linens are. But first, wipe down every single table."

The manager looks around for a moment, then makes a beeline toward the front register. He sees what he is looking for when he reaches the counter.

"Here. Catch!" he yells out to Joe.

With cat-like reflexes, Joe catches the grimy rag the manager tosses to him.

"Uh, when's the last time this thing was washed?" Joe asks.

"Washed?"

The manager cackles before he lights a cigarette and waves Joe away. Joe doesn't mind. He's already loving his independence and the money he will make every Friday on payday. He feels like he hit the jackpot.

A few hours into his shift, the lunch crowd arrives. This is when Joe discovers how hard his job actually is. Bending to clear the tables is starting to make his back ache. He doesn't have a good lifting technique and there are still two more hours to go before he gets a break.

"Who knew dishes could be so heavy," Joe says aloud to nobody in particular as he wipes down a table.

By the time he gets his first break, his feet are killing him and he is famished. One perk of the job is free food on breaks and one free meal to go after work whenever he works an eight hour shift. After he eats his meal, he heads back to work, tired and ready for a nap.

"Smile, kid. Smile!" The manager orders as Joe returns to the dining room.

Customer service is new to him. It's almost like trying to learn a new language. The customer's first. Focus on service. Collaborate with others to serve the guests. Going above and beyond. Always in a hurry. Faster, faster, faster. Joe couldn't keep up with the pace, and was fired from this job.

He learns from his mistakes, though. Over the next few years, he works as a busboy in several other restaurants, always seeking to leaving a favorable impression.

In July of 1966, Joe checks his mail. He sees a letter from the local draft board, the Selective Service. He sighs. He knows before he even opens it what it is: an order to report for an Armed Forces physical examination.

When he arrives for processing, an Army Private wearing all white hands him a long form to fill out.

"There's a water fountain over there. Keep drinking while you wait, and fill this out. Black ink only," the Private says while pointing across the room to the fountain.

"I don't have a pen. Mind if I borrow yours?" Joe asks.

"Sure. Just bring it back. It's the only one I have."

Joe assures him he'll return the pen, then takes a seat with nearly a hundred other young men who have been told to report on this day at this time. Joe scans the room as he slides into his chair.

He sees a hippie with no shoes on sitting across from him. His unwashed hair is halfway down his back and his eyes are bloodshot. He looks to be about twenty five or so. Next to him is a man in a suit. He looks like he is headed to mass, or perhaps a funeral. The expression on his face says he is nervous, and probably about eighteen years old. Three chairs down is a man who appears to be in his mid-forties. He rambles incoherently about being a World War II Veteran and not having anyone to take over his business if he's forced to return to military service.

Joe smiles to himself and fills out his form. He places the form in his seat and gets up to get a drink of water from the fountain. The water is ice cold and refreshing. Joe scans the room again as he heads to his seat. The hippie is asleep and the guy in the suit looks like he is about to have a panic attack. Joe drops his gaze to the floor and plops down in his seat again. A half hour passes before a Marine Lance Corporal escorts the entire group to the back.

"As you enter the next room, you'll hand Private Shelton your paperwork, then stand on one of the X's taped to the floor."

Joe and the others comply. They are led through a series of exercises, while the Private jots down notes.

"Now you'll each need to give a urine sample. This sample will be observed. Please follow Lance Corporal Rogers to the latrines. The observers will be there waiting."

"Observers? They're going to watch us use the bathroom?" Joe whispers to the guy wearing the suit.

"They sure are. My brother did this a few months ago. He said they stand there and watch you the whole time to make sure it's really you and you didn't bring in someone else's urine in a cup or something."

The hippie overhears this. He looks nervous now. Sweat floods his brow. This amuses Joe.

"Keep the line moving," the Private directs.

After the urinalysis, the potential inductees are sent to see various doctors, based on the first letter of their last name.

"If you last name begins with S, T, U or V, you'll fall in with Dr. Basknight," the Lance Corporal informs the group, then continues with other letters of the alphabet.

"Good luck to you," Joe smiles at the hippie.

The hippie smiles back weakly, then flashes a peace sign to Joe. Joe follows his group to Dr. Basknight. He's called first.

"Corporal, give me Saldivar's paperwork," the Doctor says without looking up from his clipboard.

The Corporal places Joe's paperwork in the Doctor's outstretched hand. The doctor scans it momentarily, then takes out his stethoscope.

"Take a deep breath and then slowly exhale while I listen."

The Doctor scribbles something.

"No tattoos. No injuries. Ok. You're…"

"Wait. I do have a couple of injuries. My knee and my ankle were injured playing football a few years ago and give me a little trouble from time to time. I put it all on the forms."

Without skipping a beat, the Doctor says "You're fit for duty. You'll report in two weeks. Get dressed and you're free to go."

The next two weeks fly by. Joe packs all of his things, drops them off in El Paso with Esperanza and then returns just in time for his liaison from the local draft board to pick him up so he can swear in at the MEPS (Military Entrance Processing Station.)

They arrive just before 7:00 AM. Joe's liaison, an Airforce Staff Sergeant, gets him signed in and then walks him to the waiting area.

"Army. Are you sure that's the branch you want?"

"One hundred percent."

Joe has given a lot of thought to which branch he wants to serve in. The Marines have it pretty rough, he has no desire to be stuck at sea for months on end in the Navy and the Air Force won't take him without a high school diploma, so Army it is. Besides, Simon had been in the Army. It seems only right that Joe would go in the Army, too, he thinks.

"I think you'll make a fine Soldier, Saldivar. Best of luck to you."

The men shake hands and Joe slips into a chair by the window and watches as the Staff Sergeant exits the room and departs the facility. Before long, an Army Captain enters the waiting room and has everyone being inducted into the Army enter a smaller room to the right.

The group piles into the room, then turns their attention to the front.

"I want everyone to raise your right hand, and then you will repeat after me."

"Yes, sir!" the group shouts in unison.

"I, state your name…"

"I, Joe Saldivar…"

"do solemnly swear that I will support and defend the Constitution of the United States against all enemies, foreign and domestic…"

Joe repeats these lines.

"That I will bear true faith and allegiance to the same, and that I will obey the orders of the President of the United States and the orders of the officers appointed over me…"

Joe repeats.

"According to the regulations and the Uniform Code of Military Justice. So help me God."

Joe stands up a little straighter, sticks his chest out and repeats.

"Welcome to the United States Army, gentlemen."

Joe smiles to himself. He inwardly beams with pride.

"Follow Sergeant Murtaugh with your bags. He'll get you on the bus to Oakland."

"Oakland?" Joe questions.

"Yes. First a bus to Oakland. In Oakland you'll catch a bus to San Francisco. Then from San Francisco we'll get you on a plane to your new home…"

"Fort Lewis Washington," Joe finishes.

Chapter Four

The trip took nearly twenty four hours. Aside from junk food they picked up at a gas station along one of the Greyhound routes, none of the inductees have eaten since lunch yesterday. It's nearly 4:00 AM. No one dares to complain. Joe is asleep when the shuttle bus from the airport pulls through the gates of Fort Lewis.

"Wake up. We're here," the guy in the seat next to Joe whispers.

Joe rubs his eyes and blinks a few times. He stretches and lets out a yawn. He notices Mt. Ranier in the distance. The sky is a vibrant hue of blue. The Ponderosa Pines and Garry Oak trees make the installation look like something you'd see on a post card. Joe wishes he had a camera so he could take a photo and send it to Esperanza.

"On your feet!" the Sergeant who accompanies them shouts as the bus rolls to a stop.

Startled, the new inductees spring to their feet in compliance. Joe glances out of the window. Soldiers are everywhere. Lots of Soldiers. He is amazed to see so many servicemen up and about at this time of morning.

"When I open this door, you have three seconds to get off this bus and form a line next to the building, on the sidewalk!"

Joe has one small bag, while the others have large bags. He weaves his arms through the straps of his bag, like a backpack. The doors open and everyone tumbles out, pushing and pulling so they can get in line within the allocated three seconds. Bags fly open, people scramble to pick up clothes. Utter chaos. But not for Joe. He's first in line, and patiently awaits further instructions.

A Drill Sergeant notices and walks up to him, standing within centimeters from Joe's face.

"What's your name, inductee?"

"Saldivar. Private Joe Saldivar."

The Drill Sergeant moves back just a bit. Joe can still feel the Drill Sergeant's breath on his face.

"Good job, Saldivar. You ever been a leader before?"

Joe freezes. He has not, but should he admit this?

"Are you hard of hearing, Saldivar? I asked you a question."

"No, sir. No I haven't."

"Sir? It's Sergeant or Drill Sergeant. Not sir. I work for a living. Got it?"

"Yes, Drill Sergeant."

"You're the new Platoon Sergeant, Saldivar. I'll give you some more guidance later. For now, get everyone on that cattle car over there in the next 30 seconds."

"Yes, Drill Sergeant!"

The Drill Sergeant takes a step back, then blows a whistle. This causes the chaotic frenzy to begin all over again. Once everyone is on the cattle car, Joe hops on.

"We're all aboard, Drill Sergeant," Joe calls out.

"Good job, Saldivar."

The Drill Sergeant closes the doors and the cattle car takes off toward the other side of the installation. Everyone stands. There are no seats. The smell of sweat and fear of the unknown fill the car. There is barely any room. The inductees stand shoulder to shoulder, face to face. The cattle car easily has sixty or seventy more people in it than it is meant to hold. Someone stands on Joe's foot, but the cattle car is so tightly packed he has no room to move his foot out of the way. Joe starts to wonder what he's gotten himself into as sweat pours from his brow.

The next several days fly by. First a haircut, then a quick call home from the pay phones to let everyone know he's made it safely. Uniforms are issued. Then weapons are issued, M14's and bayonets. The year prior, physical fitness testing had become mandatory, so they are allowed a brief trip to the Post Exchange to purchase running shoes after having pay issued to them at the end of Week One.

They had to wait in a long line with all the other Basic trainees from the other Battalions to receive their pay from the paymaster. When it is Joe's turn, he steps forward to sign for his envelope of cash from the finance clerk. He opens the envelope and counts it.

"It's all there, Private. All ninety six dollars and ninety cents. A full month's pay."

"Just making sure, Sergeant."

The finance clerk grins and waves Joe away.

He has never had a payday this large before. He's made money, but never this much all at one time. Maybe this Army thing won't be so bad after all.

In the coming days, physical training ramps up greatly.

"There's a war raging across the ocean in a tiny little country called Vietnam," the Drill Sergeant starts. "and Uncle Sam has picked you to participate. My job is to ensure you are physically prepared to engage Charlie, the enemy. My job is to ensure you are physically prepared to save the life of those standing to your left and standing to your right. My job is…" he pauses to look at each face in the group. They're all so young, he thinks.

"My job is to make sure you are physically prepared to at least stand a fighting chance of coming back home to your mommies and daddies! So I am going to work you harder than you have ever been worked in your life."

Joe snickers on the inside. He thinks about all the days he went to football practice in the blazing West Texas sun. There's nothing this Drill Sergeant can throw at him that he can't handle. The football coach at El Paso's Technical High has already worked him hard, so he is ready.

But as the days go on, Joe rethinks that mindset. Running. Jumping. Doing push-ups. Carrying all of his gear. It finally proves to be just too much for his knee on the obstacle course.

Joe races across the field and climbs over the low wall. He runs toward the next obstacle, barbed wire fencing that he has to low crawl underneath.

"You're making good time, Saldivar!" a Drill Sergeant shouts as Joe reaches the end of the barbed wire.

Joe cracks a smile and takes off, with a new burst of energy induced by his ego. He is clearly on track to finish the obstacle course with the best time.

He grabs the rope when he reaches it and uses it to climb up another wall. This one is several feet higher than the last. Instead of climbing down, he simply jumps the twelve feet or so to the other side.

"Ow!"

His knee aches, but he keeps going. As he navigates the logs, Joe falls and feels pain in his right knee. This is the same knee he injured playing football. It's so painful that he is taken right away to the hospital by the Drill Sergeants.

The doctor delivers the news that Joe's knee will only worsen with continued military service.

"We're going to have to send you home, Saldivar."

"It'll be ok. I can start over in the next class," Joe thinks out loud.

"No. We have to send you home. If we keep you in training, you'll do too much damage to it. Might not even be able to walk again."

Joe is processed for separation from the Army. There's more doctor appointments and what seems like endless paperwork. He is given an honorable discharge and a ticket back home after only ninety days.

"What's next for you, Saldivar?" the Drill Sergeant asks, sorry to see him go.

"I'm not sure, Drill Sergeant."

"What were you doing before we grabbed you up?"

"I worked as a busboy."

"So back to that?"

"I don't think so. I want something more."

Chapter Five

After he leaves the Army in November of 1966, Joe comes back to El Paso for a few months. On January 20th of 1967, he marries Bertha Acosta, whom he met four years earlier in El Paso. The couple moves to Los Angeles, California the very next day.

They soon settle into a routine. Bertha works at a manufacturing company and works hard to make a happy home for her husband.

Joe works at a number of restaurants, and even at J.J. Newberry's as a mannequin dresser, but returns to night school at

Roosevelt High. He eventually earns his high school diploma in 1969. After that, he takes general courses at East LA Junior College, as well as electrical engineering courses at LA Trade Tech. Then he works at Phillip A Hunt Chemical Corporation as a chemical mixer until 1977.

By this time, the Saldivar family has expanded. It includes twin girls and a son. The couple has left their East Los Angeles home for a place in the city of Cudahy, California. They don't want to raise their family amidst the rampant gang fights and unhealthy smog of Los Angeles.

Cudahy has one of the largest population densities of any city in the United

States. When Joe and Bertha move there, a plethora of high rise apartments are available, with more being built. They find a charming apartment that is spacious enough for their family, and surrounded by greenery. Everything seems perfect...

Joe soon begins to feel restless despite this.

"Amor, what's wrong?" Bertha asks Joe one evening.

"I don't know. I just want, well, something more."

"More? What do you mean?"

"I want to go home. Back to El Paso."

Bertha thinks on this for a moment.

"Ok. Let's do it!"

They pack their things and return to the Sun City with their children in tow. Joe finds a job at O & C Trucking, offloading trucks. He enjoys the job, but enjoys the pay even more.

After several months, however, Bertha can see he is restless. Again.

"Amor. What's the matter?"

"I'm not sure. I think I want a career change."

"All right. To what? In what field?"

Joe thinks for a moment before he answers. He takes his glasses off and carefully folds the handles in. He places them on the table before he speaks again.

"I'm thinking Corrections. I saw an advertisement that the El Paso County Jail is looking for Jailers. Maybe I can do that."

"That's a big leap from the chemical plant or unloading trucks, but I have no doubt you will find success if that is what you want."

"Yes, that is what I want."

Joe likes the idea of a new job and a fresh start. He isn't the same kid who left El Paso fourteen years ago. He's graduated high school and has a lot of life experience now. He left a boy but has returned a man. He welcomes the opportunity to work as a Jailer.

As he fills out the application, he pauses for a moment and stares at the paper.

He drops his pen on the table and gently rubs his temples.

"I'm not sure I qualify. It's asking for experience. I've always worked in restaurants."

"And the chemical plant, Amor. And unloading trucks…," Bertha reminds him.

Joe isn't convinced this is enough.

"Mira, Joe. You gained a lot of experience. Teamwork. Put that down."

"Teamwork?"

"Yes, you had to be a team with the servers to meet the customers' needs. You have to coordinate with the forklift drivers for safety when you unload the trucks. So yes, teamwork. And honesty. You can't lie to customers in the restaurant or the people on the dock as you unload trucks. They see right through you. So, honesty."

Joe scribbles down the word "honesty," then looks to Bertha.

She smiles, then leans in a little closer to Joe.

"Patience. You absolutely had to have patience. And care. You had to go above and beyond in caring for your customers to get the best tips, right? And to not damage any of the freight you unloaded on the dock, yes?"

Joe grins. He has never put any of jobs into this perspective. He's thankful for her insight. He ultimately gets the job, and enjoys it quite a bit, even though he truly wishes he could be a deputy sheriff.

To be a deputy sheriff in 1977, you have to be at least six feet tall. Joe falls a couple inches shy of that. When he starts as a Jailer, he hears rumblings that this may change. He prays it does.

After two years, Sheriff Montes launches the C.I.T.A Program. This was a program that allowed employees of the jail to transition into deputy sheriff roles. Joe is accepted into the academy under this rigorous program.

Not everyone can cut it. It's tough. Not only do they train at the academy for eight hours a day, they still work eight hour shifts as employees of the County. Plus, the El Paso County Sheriff's Office is tasked to protect approximately 1,058 square miles of land. Joe doesn't mind. The $609 a month he is paid after graduation makes the long hours incredibly worth it.

Chapter Six

Joe checks his watch. It's 3:45 PM. It's October, but true to West Texas, the sun shines brightly and the skies are a crisp blue. It's still perfect weather for short sleeves.

Joe's at the gas station at the Fabens Warehouse. He tops his patrol car off with fuel and replaces the nozzle. This fill up is on the County's dime, but he notices that gas has gone up to ninety one cents a gallon.

"Ridiculous," he says to no one in particular.

As he slides into the driver's seat, his radio goes off. Gracie Fierro, the dispatcher, requests that he comes by the substation to receive some information. He keys the microphone on his radio to acknowledge her transmission.

"I'll be there in five minutes," he tells her.

Joe hops in his car and finishes up a report he is writing. He has just arrested four teenage males who had stolen a vehicle from Las Cruces, New Mexico. He has no idea what they are doing way out here, but they are in jail now.

He starts his vehicle and drives away. When Joe arrives, Gracie beckons him over to her desk.

"I received two anonymous phone calls from a woman who states she can confirm that Juan Martinez will arrive at her home at approximately 4:00 PM."

Joe raises an eyebrow. He's intrigued.

"The woman advised me she will call the Sheriff's Department again when he arrives so that someone can come apprehend him."

"And you don't know who this woman is?"

Gracie deduces it's likely Mrs. Guillen, Juan Martinez's sister in law, who lives in the Broadway Courts apartments.

Two days prior, Juan Martinez injured two children. He, therefore, has two outstanding warrants. He severely beat the two small girls, one only seven months old. The other child was twenty-three months old. He beat the twenty-three month old so gravely that she is paralyzed on the right side of her body. Doctors have informed law enforcement the paralysis may be permanent.

Joe and the rest of the deputies are advised to exercise caution when apprehending Juan Martinez. All deputies are also informed that Juan Martinez may likely evade apprehension.

By 4:15 PM, Mrs. Guillen has still not called back. Joe remembers he needs to go back to the detention home to turn in the report relating to the stolen car incident that happened earlier in the day. He let's Gracie know he'll be back.

Joe doesn't go straight to the detention home after leaving the substation. His gut tells him to go by the Broadway Courts apartments. Apartment 25, in particular.

He knows Mrs. Guillen from previous contacts, so he decides to just check in with her to see if Juan is there. She is always pleasant, so he feels like she'll talk to him.

Joe parks his patrol unit behind a ragged car with no door, no front tires and a cracked windshield in front of Mrs. Guillen's apartment. It's clearly a junked vehicle. He'll ticket it later, he thinks. Joe slams the door of the patrol unit shut. He takes in the surroundings as he walks toward the door. Children play soccer in the street. A man and what appears to be his wife quietly argue. Another man, older, grandfatherly, sits on the hood of what Joe assumes to be his own car, drinking a forty ounce beer. The beer is still in the bag, as if that disguises what it is. Joe chuckles. That's when he notices Mrs. Guillen standing in the screen door.

"Good afternoon, Mrs. Guillen. Is Juan by any chance here?" Joe asks in low voice.

"He's not home. I'll make sure I call when he gets here."

"Do you have a telephone?"

"Yes, I do," she replies.

"If he comes in a car, please get the license plate number."

"He'll probably come with his brother Daniel, in a white car," she advises.

"Make sure you call when he arrives."

"I will. I promise."

Joe hops in his patrol car and leaves. While traveling West on North Loop, about a mile and half West of Clint, the radio crackles. It's Gracie.

"The subject Martinez is home. Officer Saldivar, please be advised."

Joe immediately calls Unit 206, which is Sergeant Fabela. Joe advises him of the two felony warrants the Sheriff's Office has for Martinez, and the amount of the bond.

"I'll send Unit two one six, Joe De la Cruz, because Unit two one two, the unit normally assigned to Fabens, is en route to an accident," Fabela responds.

Joe advises Sergeant Fabela of his location.

"Do you want me to assist Unit two one six, since I'm already over here?" Joe asks.

"Affirmative," comes the response.

Joe calls Deputy De la Cruz on the radio.

"Unit two one six, what is your location and your ETA to the subject's location in Fabens?"

"I'm on Farm Road two fifty eight. I'll be there in about five minutes."

"Meet me at the church near the substation," Joe directs.

"Copy."

At this same time, the Criminal Investigation Division is serving other warrants in the area. The Captain of CID Unit 401, Captain Bonilla, calls the dispatcher.

"I need all traffic to keep clear of the radio," he commands the dispatcher.

Within moments, Gracie calls Joe on the radio, obviously missing Captain Bonilla's commands to clear the channel.

"Disregard. Martinez is no longer there."

"So he's gone? We missed him?"

"The lady called again and just said he's no longer there."

Since Joe is fairly close to Mrs. Guillen's apartment, he decides to check in with her again to see if she at least got the license plate of the vehicle Juan Martinez is in, or knows which way he went.

When Joe arrives, he parks behind the junked vehicle again. He can see Mrs. Guillen's silhouette in the screen door once more. She motions to Joe using her eyes, her eyebrows, and gestures with her head toward the back part of the apartment, indicating Juan Martinez is actually still there with her.

"Who are you looking for?" Mrs. Guillen asks Joe in Spanish, in a voice louder than her normal tone.

Mrs. Guillen then lifts her right hand up slowly, then points with her index finger toward the back of the apartment. It is apparent to Joe that Mrs. Guillen does not want Juan Martinez to be aware that she has tipped Joe off. In response to her question, Joe hesitates before he speaks.

"I'm looking for a man, a Juan Martinez" he finally says.

Joe is concerned that Juan Martinez knows he is outside. This could lead to Martinez exiting the apartment through a rear window. Joe opens the screen door. Mrs. Guillen moves back. She neither invites him in nor prevents him from coming in. She simply steps out of the way.

Joe knows that Mrs. Guillen wishes to give the impression that she is trying to keep law enforcement at bay. She will likely have big problems from Juan or her husband if they feel like she is cooperating with law enforcement to have Martinez arrested.

Joe approaches the back bedroom on the west side of the apartment.

"No one is here!" Mrs. Guillen says loudly.

Joe sees the bed on the north wall and two small closet-like openings on the west wall. He checks the closet on the right side first because the closet on the left appears to be empty. Joe then bends down to check underneath the bed. Nothing but a few dust bunnies and two pairs of shoes lined up neatly along the edge of the bed's frame.

"No one is under the bed!" Mrs. Guillen shouts.

She looks down the hallway again toward the bathroom, then motions to Joe that Martinez is, in fact, there.

Joe takes her cues. He moves steadily toward the bathroom. He notices the shower curtain is pulled closed. At this time, he slowly draws his weapon. He opens the shower curtain even more slowly. Joe sees Martinez standing against the wall, wearing grey slacks and a grey shirt.

Even though the man before him is much larger than the description he has been provided, Joe knows immediately that this is the subject he is searching for.

"Step out very slowly," Joe commands Martinez.

"Why are you looking for me?" Juan Martinez asks in Spanish.

"I have a warrant for your arrest."

"I haven't done anything. You have no reason to look for me."

"Do you know this individual?" Joe asks Mrs. Guillen who is nervously watching the scene unfold.

"Yes. This is my brother in law. Juan Martinez."

"Lie down on the bed, Martinez," Joe commands.

"For what?"

"So that I can handcuff and search you."

"I'm not doing that. I haven't done anything!" Juan angrily argues.

"Lie down on the bed," Joe again commands.

"No. I didn't do anything."

Juan Martinez looks at Joe's gun for a moment.

"Just kill me," Martinez says.

Joe is unsure if this is a dare or a plea. He decides to take Martinez outside. There will be less of a chance of Mrs. Guillen getting injured and there might be someone outside to assist him if he needs it, Joe thinks.

Joe guides Martinez through the kitchen.

"Unit two one six," Joe calls on his radio. "What's your ETA? Officer needs assistance."

There is no response.

"Unit two one six," Joe calls again.

He tries several more times, but gets no response. The Criminal Investigation Unit is engaging in a lot of radio traffic. This may be why Joe is unable to get a response.

On the way out of the house, Martinez demands to see the warrant for his arrest.

"It's in the car. I'll show it to you," Joe lies, in hopes that Martinez will now cooperate.

All Joe has is a yellow piece of paper with Martinez's information, given to him by one of the detectives. He thinks about this for a moment. If his white lie doesn't work, he hopes back up arrives soon.

Joe and Martinez exit the apartment, as Joe continuously points his weapon at

Martinez. As they near the patrol unit, still parked behind the junked vehicle, Joe gives Martinez a few commands.

"Put your hands on top of the patrol car so I can be sure you are unarmed. I need to handcuff you."

"Go ahead and shoot me! I ain't going with you!"

Joe pushes Martinez behind his shoulder, and forces him against the patrol unit. Martinez spins toward Joe and punches him. Hard. Joe reels, but doesn't fall down. Martinez casually walks away toward the alley.

"Hey! You aren't free to leave," Joe calls to Martinez.

Martinez ignores him. Joe keys his radio and calls for assistance.

"Unit two one six. Unit two one six."

No response.

"Unit two one six, officer requests back up."

No response. Joe also calls out to the main dispatch and the substation. No response from any of them. The only thing that can be heard is radio traffic from the CID units.

Martinez heads south, across the alley, through the passageway to the section of the Broadway Courts immediately south of where he and Joe had originally been. Joe catches up to Martinez and shoves him against the west wall. Martinez tries to punch Joe in the face. Joe dodges skillfully and takes a step back. He will not allow Martinez to have access to his weapon, nor will he allow Martinez to punch him again.

Martinez then continues walking away. Joe walks side by side with him. They start to cross Main Street at the crosswalk.

A green pick-up truck stops in the crosswalk at the now red light. This gives Martinez an opportunity to dash around the truck and escape. Martinez ditches Joe and runs south, down another alleyway.

"Kill me if you want to!" Martinez screams over his shoulder as he runs away, with Joe in pursuit.

The two men continue south between some apartments. They enter an empty lot and Joe catches up to him by running parallel on the right side, approximately eight feet away. Martinez continues to run, but Joe keeps up. Joe repeatedly calls for assistance this whole time. There is no response.

It's apparent to Joe that back up is not coming. Martinez is nearing a canal, with Joe on his heels. The area is isolated. Joe notices they are mere feet from the border. He realizes that if Martinez escapes into the canal, he will elude apprehension by going into Mexico.

In a split second, Joe must decide his course of action. Joe doesn't know if this guy has a weapon or not, as he never had the chance to search him, but Martinez has his hand in his waistband and keeps looking back at Joe. Joe knows the suspect is violent because he unmercifully beat two small children, babies actually, nearly killing them both and paralyzing one of them. Not to mention he threw a mean right hook at Joe's jaw, and would have done more damage had Joe not evaded his fists. More violence is sure to ensue if Joe doesn't take action quickly.

Joe pulls his weapon, a show of force.

"Martinez, stop! Drop to one knee, then lie on the ground."

Martinez's nostrils flare as he turns to face Joe. Sweat glistens on the brow of both men.

"I'm not going to jail. Kill me if you want, but I'm not going to jail!' Martinez says as he charges toward Joe.

In that split second, Joe has to make a decision to shoot or not to shoot. Joe fears for his safety and to some degree, his life. Martinez is far larger than him, and absolutely no one is around to help if this suspect gets the best of him.

"BAM!"

Joe fires his .45 automatic once, striking Martinez on the right side of his body. Martinez's right hand shoots high in the air, over his shoulder and he spins around one hundred and eighty degrees before he falls to the ground. Joe can see Martinez is bleeding.

A pick-up truck rumbles down the road in their direction. Joe flags the driver down.

"I need you to go to the substation and call an ambulance and other deputies. No one's answering on the radio."

Joe returns to Martinez to administer first aid. Several minutes later, Unit 216, Deputy De La Cruz, arrives. Joe gives him a recap of the events that have transpired. Joe then walks back to see Mrs. Guillen.

"I just need to verify that the person I have arrested is, indeed, Mr. Juan Martinez."

"Yes, he is."

Joe gets in his patrol car and returns to Martinez. He parks close to the canal, a few feet from Martinez who is still on the ground, but being attended to by a deputy. Joe pauses just before he reaches Martinez. He's sorry blood has been spilled but he knows he did the right thing. He takes a step closer to Martinez, who reads Joe's nametag aloud.

"Saldivar. I'm going to remember you."

Joe ignores this statement.

"Turn me on my side," Juan Martinez asks.

Joe discourages this. Moving him may cause further injury. A few moments later, the ambulance arrives and takes Martinez away.

Joe is suspended pending the internal investigation. It's nearly two years later before he finds himself in court over this matter. Mr. Martinez, now paralyzed, and his wife Lourdes sue not only Joe, but the County of El Paso, Sheriff Leo Samaniego and former Sheriff Mike Davis for their professional connections to Joe.

By the time Joe gives his deposition in court, he feels like a scapegoat. He already has three disciplinary issues in the last few years, one of which earns him a five day suspension. It feels like all eyes are on him, but he remains calm and collected.

"Let's talk about the second time that you were disciplined. When was that?" the attorney asks Joe during his deposition in the Martinez lawsuit.

"...I did get a five day suspension."

"Approximately what year was that?"

"I believe about 1983," Joe responds.

"Before the Juan Martinez case? It was almost a year before the Juan Martinez shooting?"

"Maybe a little over a year. It was probably closer to two years."

"What was that suspension for?"

"…Some lady had a heart attack in Canutillo during church services. An eighty year old lady who had a history of heart conditions. This, I found out later on, through the Medical Examiner."

Joe pauses, looks around the courtroom, then proceeds.

"She died in the church of a heart attack due to the fact that an ambulance got there late. I was the dispatcher at the time. It was kind of a long story, but the ambulance did get there late."

"…you were dispatching?"

"Well, a dispatcher is still a part of the patrol division," Joe explains.

Joe and his Co-Defendants have their professional lives picked apart on the stand day after day. Ultimately, Juan Martinez is awarded $300,000+.

Chapter Seven

Nine girls and women have gone missing since February 1987 in El Paso, Texas. It's now August. Those missing are between the ages of 13 and 24. Joe shakes his head as he continues to listen to the report his Lieutenant is giving at shift change.

He thinks about his own teenage daughters. He also thinks about Marylou. Marylou played basketball at San Eli High when they first met in 1980. At the time, he worked Crime Prevention at the school. They've grown close, maybe too close, since her graduation in 1981. He worries about her safety as much as he does that of his girls and his wife. He hopes this apparent serial killer is caught soon.

The Lieutenant goes on to provide details about current, known victims.

"The first of them is fourteen year-old Marjorie Knox, who disappeared on February fourteenth," the Lieutenant shares.

Marjorie lived in Chaparral, New Mexico, a suburb of El Paso, but on that day, she had gone to the city to attend a Valentine's Day party in Veterans Park with friends.

"Three weeks later, on March seventh, thirteen year-old Melissa Alaniz also went missing. Both girls' parents knew each other, as they worked at the Rockwell Company," the Lieutenant continues.

Alaniz's parents told police that in the months prior to her disappearance, their daughter had been going through puberty and had become acquainted with a group of young men with criminal records.

On June 7, El Paso police received a report concerning the disappearance of 15-year-old Desiree Wheatley. During their investigation, several witnesses claimed that they had last seen her five days prior in the company of a man with numerous tattoos on his arms at a convenience store. Wheatley attended H.E. Charles Junior High School, lived near and was not known to consume alcohol or use drugs.

"Nearest neighbor is a David Leonard Wood. EPPD does not consider him a person of interest at this time."

Joe wonders why. Then the Lieutenant continues.

"Three days later, the police received another report about the disappearance of twenty year-old Karen Baker, who was last seen alive on June fifth, on the grounds of the Hawaiian Royale Motel. The case proved tough, as witnesses gave conflicting accounts of her actions prior to her disappearance, with her own mother claiming that she had been kidnapped and taken to Mexico, prompting the FBI to investigate her claim."

This is really bad if the FBI is involved, Joe thinks. He leans forward and hangs on to every word as the Lieutenant continues.

"On June twenty eighth, nineteen year-old Cheryl Lynn Vasquez-Dismukes, an employee at a local Whataburger, went missing in El Paso, after going to buy cigarettes at a Circle K. According to witnesses, she was last seen talking to a man in a pickup truck."

Joe wonders which Circle K. He makes a note to ask that clarifying question. He listens eagerly as the Lieutenant continues to detail how on July 3, a 17-year-old girl named Angelica Jeannette Frausto was also reported missing. The latter girl was a repeat runaway since the age of 12, and often absent from home for days and even months.

At age 15, she dropped out of Henderson Middle School before taking on a job as a dancer at Red Flame. During the investigation, police discovered that on the day of her disappearance, Frausto was given a motorcycle ride by one of her biker friends, a David Leonard Wood.

"And he's not a suspect yet?" one of the deputies interrupts.

The Lieutenant ignores him and proceeds.

"A month later, on August 20, the parents of 24-year-old Rosa Maria Casio contacted the police. They claimed that she had been visiting her sister in Ciudad Juárez on August 12, and in the evening, she went to El Paso by car to buy postage stamps, but then vanished. On the following morning, her 1974 Ford Gran Torino was found abandoned at a street, with Casio's belongings still inside it. Interviews with local residents provided no useful information relating to her vanishing."

Casio worked as a topless dancer in a bar in El Paso, but according to her parents, she was not involved in prostitution and planned to enroll in Dallas College

Brookhaven Campus to complete her education.

A month goes by, and they still haven't found the killer. Now, 14 year-old Dawn Marie Smith, a student at Parkland High School is reported missing. She had gotten into an argument with her parents in June before running away from home, saying she would never return.

She stayed in touch with some of her family, Joe reads in the shift briefing paperwork. But, it says she only stayed in touch until August 28. After that, all contact ceased.

Joe furrows his brow as he reads on. Local informants told police officers that

Smith had been shot and killed by a biker on a property in Chaparral. Law enforcement has not yet conclusively verified this information.

A few days later, Judith Kelling Brown, a prostitute and drug addict who lives in the area where women are vanishing, contacts the El Paso Police Department. She tells them that on one day between July 26 and August 7, she met a young man who lured her into his pickup truck with the promise of driving her home. According to her, the man missed the right turn and explained that he would take her back after he first visited his friend, whereupon he stopped outside an apartment building and went inside. When he returned about three minutes later, a rope was dangling from one of his pockets.

Brown claims that the man then drove her to the Northeast part of El Paso, toward the desert, in the opposite direction of where her house was. Joe wonders why Brown still left with the man, but he continues to read.

The man explained to Brown, the briefing states, that there was a shipment of cocaine buried there and he had to get it, and after some time, he stopped the truck, got out, and told her to exit as well. He then pulled a blanket and shovel from the back of the truck, and then tied her to the vehicle at gunpoint. After digging a hole in the ground, he proceeded to rape her before attempting to strangle her but could not finish as some passers-by were approaching. The man then took Kelling to another spot in the desert and raped her at gunpoint again, but as passers-by interrupted again, he abandoned her and fled.

Joe is disgusted that the passers-by did nothing. He keeps reading. Kelling indicated to law enforcement on a map the alleged location of the attack and was asked to look at five photographs of criminals convicted of similar crimes in the past. One of the men was David Leonard Wood, whom she positively identified as her assailant.

Wood should now officially be a suspect, but he isn't. Why? Joe thinks to himself.

"Yeah, I want to catch this guy, too. They just don't have enough evidence," another deputy says when he sees Joe reading the briefing.

A few weeks later, hikers accidentally discover the remains of Wheatley and Smith, both of whom are buried in shallow graves close to one another and about 1.5 kilometers away from those of Casio and Baker. The location where they are found matches the area where Kelling testified that she had been attacked by Wood, finally making him an official suspect in the murders.

"So this Saturday, gentlemen, we'll be out in Northeast El Paso, working with the El Paso Police Department and maybe even the FBI to scan the desert."

"And what exactly are we looking for?" Joe asks.

"Corpses…"

It is an incredibly hot day. So hot, Joe thinks someone might pass out as they walk the desert. The deputies look for low areas that have sunk due to soil compression. They look for differences in ground cover. Things like dead plants or evidence of recent digging. Cadaver dogs guide humans across the rough terrain. They are specially trained to detect the smell of decomposing human flesh. In terms of cost, speed, efficiency and accuracy, nothing beats them. Ground penetrating radar is also used as the deputies hunt for buried human remains.

The deputies stay alert for coyotes and buzzards.

"Animals can be helpful in locating dead bodies," Joe shares with one of the newer deputies.

There's a sea of law enforcement officers spread across the area near Rushing and further north, in the Northeast part of the city, for more than twelve hours. They don't find anything. This time.

David Leonard Wood is eventually convicted of his crimes against Kelling. He was already on parole for two other rapes, and this is an aggravated crime. He receives a sentence of fifty years. A few years later, with better science and more evidence, Wood will be yanked from his prison cell, tried for six of the murders and receive a death sentence.

Chapter Eight

Joe is now working the Upper Valley Sector, on the west side of the Franklin Mountain, near Vinton. His partner has just responded on the radio to a call about an aggravated kidnapping.

"En route…"

"10-4"

Joe flips on his emergency lights and heads toward Kiely Road. As they reach the apartment complex, Joe and his partner see a vehicle speeding away. Joe does a sharp U-turn and follows the vehicle closely.

"Call in a chase," Joe directs his partner, who complies.

Joe and his partner attempt to pull the vehicle over several times.

"He's just blowing us off. Totally ignoring the lights and all," Joe says in disbelief.

The dispatcher calls them on the radio.

"The Complainant states kidnapper is the father of the ten year old girl. He plans to take her into Juarez and the Complainant, the mother, is worried he will not return her."

Joe and his partner give each other a knowing look. They are less than three miles from the crossing into Juarez. Their attention shifts when the driver of the vehicle slows down and slams on the brakes.

Not wanting to crash, Joe veers to the side of him and slows to a halt. The suspected kidnapper then puts his car back in gear and sideswipes Joe's patrol car, attempting to run him off the road.

Joe flicks a switch. Now his sirens are on. The suspect continues to attempt ramming Joe and his partner off the road, but Joe stays in full pursuit. Suddenly, the driver takes a hard left on Vinton Road.

"Suspect heading west on Vinton Road," Joe's partner calls out on the radio.

Joe pulls up to the vehicle and attempts to slow him down. The driver instead chooses to sideswipe the patrol car again.

"Now he's making a left, headed south, on Highway twenty eight," Joe's partner calls out over the radio.

Back up has arrived. They, too, are in hot pursuit of the suspect, right behind Joe's patrol car. The suspect looks in his rear view mirror. He sees the officers behind him.

"Daddy! I want to go home!" the little girl cries.

"Shut up!" he retorts in Spanish, as he continues to eye the officers in the rear view mirror.

He mashes the accelerator to the floor and makes a hard right onto a wide dirt road. Joe follows, as does the other patrol unit. Dust engulfs all three cars. Visibility crashes to zero for a moment. When the dust cloud settles, the suspected kidnapper is nowhere to be seen. The second patrol car keeps speeding south. Joe makes the decision to turn right.

"There he is!" Joe exclaims.

He sees the suspect sliding all over the road before the vehicle finally stops. Joe speeds up. He slams the car into park and with the engine running, Joe and his partner hop out, weapons drawn.

"Exit the vehicle!" Joe yells.

The man fails to comply. Joe runs around on the driver's side and his partner runs around on the passenger's side. They try to open the doors, to no avail. The suspect revs his engine.

"BAM! BAM! BAM! BAM!"

Joe and his partner shoot the suspect's tires out before running back to their patrol car. The chase is on again. They follow the suspect at high speed for about two blocks before they are forced to slow down.

"I'm stuck!" Joe shouts out to his partner.

The dirt road has proven too much for the patrol unit, but Joe keeps the suspect in sight.

"There it goes!" Joe says with excitement after a few minutes of spinning his wheels and breaking free of the dirt.

Joe gives chase again and catches up to the suspect. A wrestling match ensues between the suspect, Joe and Joe's partner. Moments later, they are joined by other El Paso County Sheriff's deputies. New Mexico State Police are also on the scene by this time. They finally gets handcuffs on the suspect.

"Put him in the back of my car," Joe says to one of the responding deputies, as he walks toward the New Mexico State Police Officers to thank them for their help. As they chat, they hear glass shatter.

"What the heck?" Joe says as he turns toward his patrol unit.

The suspect has kicked out the back window in Joe's patrol car and tries to escape.

He is quickly captured and Joe hands him over to the New Mexico State Police.

"I'll let you all do the paperwork since it happened in your jurisdiction," Joe teases.

"How kind of you," one of the New Mexico State Police Officers retorts sarcastically.

They all laugh.

Another New Mexico State Police Officer holds and consoles the crying ten year old girl.

Joe walks toward his patrol car. He looks at his partner.

"I could use a good meal right about now."

"Yeah. Me, too."

They hop in their car and head back toward El Paso.

Chapter Nine

Joe does a lot of moonlighting. If he isn't working security at the Fabens Recreation Center, he often works security at the coliseum for concerts.

Tonight, he works a concert. It's an easy gig. People just come to listen to the music and have a good time. No one wants trouble, particularly not law enforcement.

"Hey, who's that kid over there?"

"What kid?" Joe replies to the deputy he is working with.

"That one. The one throwing that Levi jacket up in the air over and over."

"Oh. That's Richy. Richard Ramirez. He's harmless. He's always at these concerts, tossing that jacket in the air. You don't need to worry about him, but I would keep my eye on that drunk in the row behind him."

The concert ends without anyone getting arrested.

"I'll see you later. I have an early shift tomorrow," Joe tells his colleague.

The next morning Joe is up bright and early. He is on patrol in Clint, and he expects this Saturday morning to be just as uneventful as the concert he had worked the night before. He pulls up in the left turn lane behind another car at the light on Alameda, going east bound. The light cycles a few times, but the driver doesn't turn. A call comes through on the radio, so Joe decides to go around the car and head left on FM 1110.

As Joe turns, CRASH! Seemingly out of nowhere, a vehicle plows into Joe's patrol vehicle. Joe feels the impact and becomes dizzy. Within seconds, he passes out. Chaos ensues. The driver of the car Joe has gone around jumps out and frantically tries to revive Joe, to no avail. He then sprints across the street to the grocery store.

"Someone, call for help! A deputy has been in a bad accident outside. The people in the other car are hurt, too!"

Graciela's husband works as a deputy for the El Paso County Sheriff's Office. Her heart skips a beat. What if it's him? She sprints outside and over to Joe. She is relieved it is not her husband, but sad to see Joe there, knocked out.

"Sir! Sir! Can you hear me? Sir!"

Joe's struggles to open his eyes. Once they are open, it's hard to focus. He's still in his patrol car. He's been knocked somehow out of the driver's seat, across the radio assembly, and into the passenger's seat. The driver's side window is smashed out and glass is everywhere. Joe had bounced off of it and it shattered before he was slammed into the passenger seat. Joe sees the woman outside his patrol car.

"Ma'am, please help me out," Joe winces, feeling the need to take control of the scene.

"Just stay still. The ambulance is on the way. My manager called for help."

Joe passes out again. When he comes to, he is in the ambulance. Two patrolmen have arrived. They take witness statements near the ambulance. Joe can hear the patrolmen's questions, but he doesn't hear any responses.

"I didn't see a stop sign there," Joe blurts out to the EMT, who looks confused.

Of course you didn't, Joe immediately thinks to himself. You were at a light. They don't put stop signs where traffic lights are, Joe tells himself aloud.

By the time Joe makes it home from the hospital, he is more alert, but incredibly sore. He looks himself over in his bathroom mirror. His face is completely covered in bruises.

"Nothing to see here," he jokes to himself. "Just another day at the office."

Joe heals and eventually goes to a 3 PM to 11 PM shift. One December day, just as it's getting dark, around 5 PM, he is on duty in the San Elizario area.

"Family fight in progress in Fabens. Need you to assist," the dispatcher's voice blares from Joe's radio.

"Copy."

The dispatcher gives the address and Joe flips his lights on. He continues driving west on Socorro Road in the left lane. Another vehicle is also traveling west bound, but in the right lane. This driver makes the decision to turn left, directly into Joe's patrol car.

"What the…!" Joe screams as he loses control and crashes.

At full force, the other driver's car has collided into Joe.

"Dispatcher, be advised I've been involved in a traffic accident near San Eli High. The perpetrator made an illegal left turn and crashed into my unit…"

Joe describes the scene to the dispatcher in detail before he exits his patrol car. He assesses the damage, then sighs. He walks toward the other vehicle.

"Son of a…"

Joe moves in close to the vehicle for a better look. Then he looks to his left, then his right. He spins in a circle. The other driver isn't there. Joe walks back toward his patrol unit. That's when he notices a seemingly intoxicated person walking toward El Rebote Bar at 12190 Socorro Road. The bar is approximately a hundred yards from the high school. The bar was built long before the high school. In fact, it's probably about a hundred years old. That's why it has been grandfathered in and allowed to remain so close to a school.

"Hey!" Joe calls out to him.

The man doesn't acknowledge him and keeps walking. Joe isn't sure if the man is ignoring him, or doesn't hear him. The man reaches the door and pauses. Joe is hopeful he will turn around.

"Achoo!"

The man sneezes, then enters the bar. Joe can't believe his eyes.

"You son of a…"

Joe dashes across the street and into the bar. He scans the room. It's a dingy, low-life dive. Wooden bar stools line the counter. The tables and booths are crowded, and the waitstaff overworked. Tejano music blares from a jukebox in the corner. Glasses clink, cutlery scrapes plates, and the scent of greasy, spicy food, cigarettes, too much after-shave and bad breath fills the air. Joe's stomach wretches.

He locks eyes with his suspect. The man is seated at the worn and haggard looking bar, with one elbow on the counter and a drink in hand. He sees Joe and gulps down the liquid.

Smoke permeates the room and Joe is forced to adopt a squint. He walks toward the suspect and yanks him off the bar stool and onto his feet. The drunk trucker on the next stool springs up, knocking a collection of empty beer mugs off the bar.

"Damn it!' the bartender yells.

Joe drags the uncooperative suspect toward the door. A woman with platinum blonde hair and a tight mini skirt blocks his way. She eyes Joe like a lioness, hungry to annihilate a predator. She grasps the beer bottle in her hand more tightly.

Before she can make another move, with one hand, Joe gently moves her out of the way and kicks the door open.

"I didn't do nothin'!" the suspect shouts as Joe guides him toward the accident scene with a firm grip on his shoulder.

"Yeah, you did something. You see that?" Joe says, exasperated as he points to his patrol car.

The man giggles.

"You're under arrest, sir. Place your hands behind your back."

Joe clicks the handcuffs in place, then pats the now compliant subject down. He has no weapons.

"Oye! Pendejo!"

"This accident is your fault, not his!"

Joe turns to face the direction of the bar. Three men, one with a chain in his hand, walk toward him. They are quite clearly intoxicated.

"Oh brother," Joe says to himself. "Just another day at the office," he thinks as he throws the suspect into the back of the patrol car, jumps in and drives away.

Chapter Ten

The phone rings for the fifteenth time this evening. Bertha stomps to the phone and answers it. She clenches her jaw before she speaks. She wishes she had taken it off the hook after the last call.

"Bueno!"

No response, but she hears breathing.

"Hello…?"

The line goes dead. Moments later, the phone rings again.

"I've got it, Mom," one of the twins yells.

She grabs the phone from her mother.

"Listen, whoever you are, stop crank calling our house. My dad is a cop."

"I know and he's so sexy!" the caller yells before breaking out into a raucous laughter and slamming down the phone.

"It's the middle of the night. Why isn't daddy home to deal with this?" one of the twins asks.

"Yeah, he's never worked nights before. Why all of a sudden now?" the other twin daughter asks.

"And weekends! He never worked weekends before. He never seems to even have an off day now. And this all started the same time these crank calls did…"

Bertha is not sure what to say, so she says nothing. Her gut tells her it's that woman people have been telling her about. The woman Joe is supposedly having an affair with down in San Eli. Her stomach turns flips and her heart breaks just thinking about it.

They haven't been arguing, she thinks. She tells him she loves him often, just as he tells her. She cooks, she cleans, she irons the clothes... He pays the bills, buys them nice things, makes sure the children have everything they need for school...

"Why would he cheat?" she asks herself aloud.

She snaps out of her thoughts as she realizes the girls are watching her. Her son, too.

"Let's get ready for bed. You all have school tomorrow and I want you to get a good night's rest," Bertha tells her kids.

The next day while the children are at school, Bertha calls Joe's sister Celia. They discuss the crank calls and whisperings of Joe's affair.

"I'll pick you up and show you the girl I think it might be. But I don't want any trouble. Remember, I live down here in San Eli. I have to see these people again."

"I understand. No trouble. I promise," Bertha tells her in Spanish.

They pass by the woman's house slowly.

"That's her. Marylou," Celia points.

Bertha catches a glimpse.

"This girl's just a child. It can't be her…" Bertha says, incredulous.

Celia places her hand atop Bertha's, to comfort her. They ride in silence back to El Paso. Bertha's almost certain Joe is not having an affair with this Marylou girl. She's too young, Bertha thinks. Barely older than their seventeen year old girls.

"He's having an affair with someone, though," Bertha says to herself as she prepares dinner for the kids.

Her children be home soon from school. The phone rings and startles Bertha, who is lost in her thoughts.

"Hello."

"Bertha, I hate to be the bearer of bad news…"

Her friend, the wife of another deputy, shares a rumor with Bertha. Apparently, Joe has been using his assigned undercover car to keep his affair a secret.

"What! That's why he never argues about me keeping the van anymore. Ok. Go on…"

Bertha's heartbreak blurs with fury. Her friend goes on to let her know that rumor has it Joe can be found on many nights at

McGee's Night Club. In fact, a few wayward husbands are known to frequent McGee's.

'Thanks, my friend. I'll let you know what happens."

"It's just not right, Bertha. I'm so sorry…"

Bertha is shaking by the time she hangs up the phone. Her heart rate increases and a single tear falls to her cheek.

"Mom? You good?"

The twins are home.

"Yes, dear. I'm fine."

The girls look at each other. They can see that their mother is not fine.

"Mom? What's going on?"

Bertha hesitates for a moment. She looks into the eyes of her beautiful girls. They are young women, with hopes, dreams and lots of love to give. She would never want them to experience the heartbreak their father is putting her through. She realizes at this moment that Joe's cheating will only serve to cause her children heartbreak, too. How could he do this to them? She takes a deep breath before she speaks.

"I think your father may be having an affair. Tonight, I'm going to find out. I know where he might go."

The girls are not surprised. They have had their own suspicions.

"You can't go alone, Mom. I'll go with you."

"And I'll watch Joey."

The phone rings. It's Joe.

"Just calling to say hello," he tells Bertha.

She isn't sure how to respond.

"Hello. I, uh, I'm here with the kids, about to eat dinner…"

Bertha makes small talk, but internally, she soothes her fast breaking heart.

Later, Bertha makes sure her make up is on point and her hair is perfectly coiffed. She sprays an extra spritz of her favorite perfume, the one Joe loves so much. She wants him to know what he has at home. Around Midnight, Bertha and her daughter drive to McGee's.

Bertha gasps out loud as she pulls into the parking lot of the night club.

"That's daddy's undercover car," her daughter says, almost in a whisper.

They both stare at the car for a moment before Bertha finds a spot and pulls in.

"Want me to go in with you?"

"You can't. You aren't old enough. I'm patient. I'll sit here and wait for him to come out."

A few hours later, Bertha sees her husband. She nudges her daughter.

"Stay here. I'll be right back, mija."

Her daughter exits the car anyway. Bertha makes a beeline for Joe, who still has his arm around Marylou's waist.

"What are you doing, Joe? She's a child for God's sake! How can you do this to our family…"

As Joe rebelliously listens to his wife's tirade, he sees his daughter out of the corner of his eye.

"Marylou! Run!" he shouts.

It's too late. His daughter tackles Marylou and lays into her like a pro boxer. Joe attempts to break it up.

"Don't you walk away from me, Joe!"

The next morning, Joe slides into bed, still pretending he's been at work all night and acting as if nothing has happened.

"You have nothing to say for yourself, Joe?"

Bertha sits up, her heart now shattered. In this moment, she hates him…but she loves him.

Joe says nothing for a few moments.

"Listen, we have a good marriage. We really do. I just don't feel anything for you anymore."

"What?"

Bertha is confused. What Joe just said makes zero sense.

"I don't feel anything for you anymore. Nunca. Not a thing. The more time I've spent with Marylou, the more I realized I don't care about you. Plain and simple."

"Joe, please don't do this. Think of the kids. We've been happy for twenty one years!"

"I don't feel anything for you. It's over. I'm glad you found out."

Joe marries Marylou in a huge church wedding in San Elizario, a few months after his divorce to Bertha is final. His children are heartbroken, confused and angry, as is Bertha, but he feels no compassion for them. Later he will, but not right now. Right now, he simply feels…nothing. He justifies the rift by citing all the times he had to work and couldn't spend too much time at home. His children and Bertha attribute it to his affair. Joe and Marylou welcome their own son three years later.

Chapter Eleven

Joe still suffers from the injuries he received in that last car accident. His right arm hurts so badly he finally decides to visit a doctor.

"You're going to need surgery and several months of physical therapy," the doctor informs Joe.

"You could tell all that from two x-rays?" Joe teases.

"Yes, you'll be off work for four or five months."

It turns out that Joe is off work longer. His foot was also swelling and giving him problems, so he had to have foot surgery, as well. He finally comes back to work more than six months later.

"Hey, remember that kid Richy? What was his last name?"

"Ramirez," Joe responds, not looking up from the situation report he is reading.

"Yeah, that's it. Ramirez. Richard Ramirez. Did you know they picked that kid up in LA for being a serial killer?"

Joe drops the paper he is reading and looks up from his seat in shock.

"He always seemed like a good kid," Joe quips.

"I guess he was til he wasn't. They say he was committing robberies, home invasions, rapes and, well, murders."

"A darn shame. He had a lot of potential."

It's Joe's first day back at work. The Supervisor assigns him to the Fabens area.

"Fabens has been real slow on calls lately. You should have an easy day, Joe."

"Let's hope so!" Joe says with a smile.

About an hour into his shift, Joe receives a call from the dispatcher about a man who has stolen a washing machine from his mother.

"His mother?"

"Yes, his mother."

Joe looks at his partner and they both shake their heads. The dispatcher continues.

"Meet the Complainant, the woman's other son, at the store near Tornillo."

"10-4."

When Joe arrives at the store, he sees the Complainant, a tall, lanky man in jeans with work boots on, standing in the parking lot, just as he said he would be. Joe backs into a parking space. He looks around as he and his partner exit. A car passes by, but no people really seem to be out, not even at this grocery store. Perhaps it will be a quiet day, indeed, Joe thinks to himself.

"Good evening, sir. You wanted to make a report about a washing machine?"

The man gives details about how his mom and brother have basically been arguing so the brother went and took the washing machine from the mother's house.

"Did he buy the washing machine? This sounds like a civil matter," Joe interjects.

His partner agrees.

"Hey! That's him! That's my brother! Can you just go talk to him? Please!"

The deputies turn their attention to where the man frantically points. A truck heads down the roadway, with a washing machine loaded into the bed.

"Come on," Joe tells his partner.

They finally stop the suspect a few blocks away.

"Good evening, sir. I need your driver's license and registration, please."

"¿Qué? No hice nada."

"Yeah? No one I stop ever does anything. You're all innocent."

Joe places the man under arrest and puts him in the back of his patrol unit.

"We should call for backup. This is getting a little messy," Joe's partner says.

"Agreed."

Joe contacts the dispatcher, and backup arrives soon thereafter.

The Complainant makes his way, with two friends, over to Joe and the others.

"Let me get your brother out of the back of my car so we can sort this out."

Joe opens the door and lets the suspect out. The man immediately attempts to flee. The Complainant and his friends are able to get in his way and prevent his escape. Joe rushes to his patrol car and calls for more back up.

"Units are on the way," the dispatcher advises.

"He's running!" Joe's partner yells, in pursuit.

Joe slams the door of the patrol car shut and takes off on foot after the subject. The man leaps a chain link fence like a gazelle. Joe is right behind him, like a cheetah after its prey.

"Damn it!"

As Joe scales the fence, he slices his thumb open. He doesn't let the subject out of his sight and keeps going. A few yards later, he and his partner are able to tackle the man in the dirt and place him under arrest.

As they escort the now handcuffed man back to their patrol car, Joe sees that there are ten men in close proximity who are trying to help the suspect evade arrest.

"Thank God we called for more back up," Joe's partner states.

"Definitely."

As they near the patrol car, they count ten men who fight not only with the Complainant, but with the additional deputies who have arrived. They are in a literal physical altercation. Someone punches a deputy in the face. Another one of the deputies sprays the men with pepper spray. The wind carries it right to Joe's face and his partner's nostrils.

Joe and his partner must keep their composure. They have to escort the handcuffed man to their patrol car and place him in the back. If they take time to tend to their pepper spray inflicted ills, the man might flee again. So they keep walking.

A Border Patrol officer arrives on the scene. He sees Joe's expression and that of his partner. One whiff of the air and he knows what has happened. He tosses Joe a bottle of water. Then one to his partner.

"For your eyes."

"Thanks."

Joe looks over at his partner who is on the other side of the patrol unit, flushing out his eyes and nose with water.

"So much for a quiet day…" Joe quips.

Chapter Twelve

As Joe leaves work at the Sheriff's Office, he runs into his old friend Chevo Quiroga. The two had been great friends at El Paso Tech High and Coldwell Elementary School. Though not as close as they once were, they still kept in touch.

"¿Que Paso?" Joe asks his friend.

"Estoy van. Gracias. And you?"

"I just got transferred to the Crime Prevention Unit," Joe shares.

"That's great, Joe. I hope you can help San Elizario, because they are having a lot of problems with the Stoners and the Barrio Virgins gangs. They are causing so many problems! Lots of street fights. In school and out."

"Thanks, Chevo. I will look into it. I've gotta run, but good talking to you. I'll see you later."

Later in the week, Joe heads down to San Elizario High School. He heard they were having a meeting to find solutions to the gang problem Chevo had made him aware of. Parents are already in the Cafeteria before he arrives.

"This is the fifth burglary on our block this week!" one of the mothers shares.

She is furious.

"I've had it!" her companion exclaims.

"But what are we to do? If we testify against these gangs, they become more violent."

"And if we don't, they still become more violent."

Joe enters the building and the chatter stops. He is working Crime Prevention at the school and he wants to take this opportunity to chat with parents. As he walks to the front, he can hear parents whispering about him and pointing. He can feel them mocking him.

They think it is a joke of sorts to have a Crime Prevention Deputy stationed at the school, yet still have a rampant gang and crime problem in the area. Joe is not the first deputy to come, and the parents think he will not be the last. But the gangs? The gangs will not come and go. They are clearly here to stay.

"What are you even here for?" an agitated parent still in his work clothes asks Joe.

"I heard you were having a meeting about these gangs. That you are having a lot of problems down here at the high school."

The mocking of Joe and the Sheriff's Department picks up steam again. Joe ignores it.

"What I know for a fact is this. Each time your kids get arrested, none of you parents wants to prosecute them. We're forced to let them go."

"Ok. So what do *you* want to do to help us? Other deputies have worked here and done nothing. What will you do?" a frustrated parent asks.

"Well, if the students want to fight and get hurt, let them play a football game instead," Joe responds.

"And then…?" a parent asks.

"Tell them to go ahead and play their football game. You parents of the Barrio Virgins, tell them that the Stoners challenge the Barrio Virgins to play football. And then you, the parents of the Stoners, tell them that the Barrio Virgins challenge the Stoners," Joe says.

The parents think on this.

"But don't mention my name. If they find out this was the idea of a Sheriff's Deputy, they might not want to play. Thanks for your patience. Let's pray everything works out," Joe says before he leaves.

A few days later, Joe goes to visit a couple of the San Elizario school administrators to let them know about the football game.

"Hello Mr. Tellez and Mr. Parra. I talked to the parents about the San Elizario students, and about planning a football game. The Stoners and the Barrio Virgins will play each other," Joe tells the men.

Mr. Parra motions for Joe to have a seat.

"Ok, Joe. If the parents agree, then it's ok. But what about security?" Mr. Tellez asks.

"I'll get in touch with some deputies that will be off and have them help me out," Joe assures the men.

"Ok, Joe. Be careful," Gilbert Tellez tells him before they part ways.

Later in the week, Joe visits with the Principal at San Elizario High School, Mr. Miller. Mr. Miller has heard about the football game Joe has planned and he is concerned. Gang members playing a football game? It's unheard of. It sounds It sounds more like an alternate version of Westside

Story than reality for a small town like San Elizario.

"Joe, can you really handle this? More importantly, though, will you have security for the game?"

"Yes, sir. I have already spoken with a few police officers and they said they will help me out. Don't worry. I'm positive we can handle it."

Mr. Miller's gut doesn't feel so sure.

"We'll see you at the game, Mr. Miller!" Joe says as he leaves the office.

Joe also meets with the Socorro Optimist Club, of which he is a member, about the game. The members all pledge their support.

"Whatever you need, consider it done."

When Game Day Saturday finally arrives, Joe wakes up early. He is excited. He quickly gets dressed and leaves in his van. His twin daughters accompany him. They will serve hot dogs and sodas to the players and spectators. When they arrive, the girls are not impressed.

"The field is bare. There's no grass," one says, observing the yellowish, dried up clay.

"It looks really hard. Harder than concrete. I hope nobody actually gets tackled."

Joe agrees.

"Stay over here by the tree. The rest of the Optimist Club members will be here soon to set up the grill."

Joe walks around the field, inspecting the area. He waves to a few of the off duty patrolmen who have come to assist with security.

"Here they come," one of the deputies says as he nods his head toward the parking lot.

The Stoners players walk in side by side, shoulder to shoulder, like the Rock stars they think they are. They all wear matching black t-shirts and pants. Their parents and girlfriends cheer wildly for them. Someone in their crowd is playing music from a boom box, making their entrance that much more noticeable.

"Let's see if they play as good as they look," Joe laughs.

A few minutes later, Joe sees the Barrio Virgins group arriving to the field. Their clothing is an assortment of whatever was hanging in their closet this morning. Some have on cut off khaki pants. Some have on jeans. Everyone has on a different color shirt. Joe notices that no one on either team is wearing any protective gear. Joe and the other off duty deputies separate the boys on the field, by team.

"You, you and you, over here," Joe calls to a few of the boys on the Stoners team, while another deputy calls over some boys from the Barrio Virgins team.

Each boy's face is contorted in a frown. Joe isn't sure if this is a sign of aggression toward the other team, or a representation of how they feel about the substandard field. They're respectful to the five deputies that are on the field with them, so Joe says nothing about their frowns.

"Just a few rules, gentlemen," Joe begins.

The players all turn their attention to Joe.

"The referees are not going to put up with your bullshit today. Watch your temper.

We will definitely haul your butts away from here if you don't. Understand?"

The boys all indicate that they understand with either a head nod, ok sign or a verbal statement. So Joe continues.

"And have fun."

Not a single boy cracks a smile. They all still kept a frown on their face. One of the deputies removes a quarter from his pocket.

"Time for the coin toss."

The Stoners call tails and the Barrio Virgins call heads.

"Tails!" the deputy shouts, as nearly two hundred people look on in the stands.

The boys look around to one another, but don't say a word. The deputy continues.

"Stoners. You'll have possession of the ball first. Shake hands with the opposing team."

"Click!"

A photographer from one of the news outlets snaps a photo. Then another.

"Click!"

The boys do not shake hands, and they keep frowns secure upon their faces. The Stoners take the East Field and the Barrio Virgins take the West Field. The Stoners snap the football. The quarterback pauses for a moment, to get his bearings. He sees a teammate run halfway to the other end of the field. He knows good and well he cannot generally throw that far, but he does so anyway. He hurls the ball with all his might, and it sails less than ten yards down the field. The Barrio Virgins take the opportunity to intercept it, and all Hell seems to break loose. The rules of football no longer apply. It's literally every man for himself.

Every time the ball flies, so do cuss words, vicious elbows, feet and fists. The referees spend more time breaking up on-field fights than calling plays. Each down causes a dog pile and a flare of aggression. The referees yank the boys apart every time by their t-shirts, pants or anything else they can grab as the enraged players shriek profanities at one another.

"Shut up and get back on your team's side!" a deputy commands.

Some of the players resort to biting other players to get their points across. The deputies are vigilant, though, and keep a major knock-down-drag-out fight from happening. At half time, the score is zero to zero and the boys get a twenty minute break.

As the boys return from break, the deputies notice they are moving with a little less spring in their step than before. Their muscles ache and some can barely move. They are covered in sweat, blood and dirt.

The ball snaps. The center sends the ball sailing toward the quarterback for the Stoners. Receivers, running backs and linemen start making contact. It's a free for all on the field…

"You mother-"

"Watch your mouth!" a deputy yells.

A few minutes later someone bites another player's arm. That player bites his own teammate shortly thereafter.

"What in the world?" a deputy laughs.

A few of the dignitaries in the stands give an amused chuckle, as well. By the time the game ends, no one has scored.

"What lesson did we learn today, guys?" Joe asks the players.

They stare at him, defeated by sore muscles, bite wounds, bruises and over-active egos.

"No one is better than the other one. That was the lesson for the day, fellas."

They continue to give Joe a blank stare.

"Who's hungry?"

They come alive with this question.

"Go grab something to eat from the Optimist Club table over there. They're waiting on you."

As Joe's daughters help pass out food and drinks, he notices the boys' anger has cooled. They are mingling with one another and talking. By the time they finish their meal, some even shake hands. A few tend to each other's wounds.

"Today was a good day, Joe."

"It sure was," he tells the deputy.

Joe watches as the deputy walks to his car, gets in and drives away.

Today really is a good day, Joe thinks to himself as he helps pack up the food. If only everyday produced the lesson of no one being better than anyone else, half his job would be so much easier. Life itself would be easier he thinks.

A week after the game, Al Hinojos from CBS Channel 4 presents a Spirit of El Paso Award to Joe in front of Lorenzo G. Alarcon Elementary School. Crime at the high school and in the area has dropped about 75%. It appears it just might stay this way for a while. The award is presented to people who make a positive impact within the community. Reducing crime that much is definitely a remarkable impact.

"I'm so grateful for everyone who assisted me in making this happen," Joe says when presented with the award. He adds that "I wish I could name them all, but I just can't. Too many too name. But thanks to the Socorro Optimist Club, the deputies and everyone else."

Joe is human. He has made mistakes he had to learn painful lessons from. But above all else, he has absolutely devoted his life to making a positive impact in the community. The award is not just about a football game. It's about a life of service to

others, a path Joe would gladly pick again.

Epilogue

There was an incident where another deputy accused an inmate of exposing himself to her. A second inmate approached Joe, telling him it was another inmate, not the one being accused. Joe didn't have time to get the full story, so he told the inmate in Spanish "Ok, we'll talk about this later."

Someone else at the jail interpreted this to mean Joe had made "a deal" with the inmate, and the two planned to hash out the details later. This occurred at a time when corruption was high in departments like those in Los Angeles and other big cities. America's eyes were on law enforcement, so

Sheriffs and Police Chiefs around the country showed no mercy for infractions, whether real or imagined. Perception was thought to be reality. Joe was reprimanded and lost his Sergeant's stripes. He was unable to successfully appeal the action.

Despite this painful blow, Joe continued to dedicate the rest of his adult life to protecting and serving others. He left the El Paso County Sheriff's Office in 1994 after seventeen years of service and tried his hand at several other things

He first opened a pizza shop in Juarez. Two of his buddies from the Sheriff's Office partnered with him. Between the employees robbing him blind and vendors submitting bogus payment invoices, Joe decided to close the shop after just a year.

Joe also worked for a time as a teacher's assistant, as did his wife Marylou. While working as a teacher's assistant, he sometimes did landscaping for extra money. Later, he and his wife opened J & M Sports Cards and Toys. The business continues to thrive at the time of this writing. So does Joe.

He prays his life can be seen as a cautionary tale in some places, and an example of goodness in others. He hopes to inspire others to "want something more" and always pursue their goals and dreams, while leaving a trail of love and kindness in the world.

Joe Saldivar at his store in 2024

Joe, #84; 1962 El Paso Tech High

El Paso's Technical High, 1962

Newspaper clipping when Joe received

the Spirit of El Paso award

Joe as a Crime Prevention Officer

Joe at a Crime Prevention Event

ABOUT THE AUTHOR

Michelle Murray, a native Texan, is a screenwriter, novelist and author of children's books. She is a combat Veteran of the United States Army. Her resume credits include tv, film, the stage and books, as well as a wealth of magazine articles. She holds an undergraduate degree in Entertainment Business and an MFA in Creative Writing. She enjoys hearing from readers. You can contact her/give her feedback by emailing her at info@kmpentertainment.org

You can keep up with her projects by going to her company's website www.kmpentertainment.org or via Facebook at the KMP Entertainment page, https://www.facebook.com/KMPEntertainment/

Kendal Murray designed the cover for the book. Kendal is a Media Designer and professional actor. His resume credits include numerous episodes of television, film and the stage for his acting, and corporate clients and novelists for his media designs. Kendal holds an undergraduate degree in Entertainment Business, a Master of Fine Arts in Media Design and he is a graduate of the New York Film Academy's Acting Conservatory.